# The Scarlet Letter

Nathaniel Hawthorne

Curriculum Unit

Michael A. Benedict

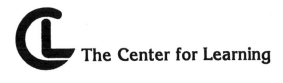

Michael A. Benedict, who earned his M.Ed. at Duquense University in Pittsburgh, PA, is English department chairperson at Fox Chapel Area High School. He is a 1989 Christa McAuliffe Fellow and a Fellow at the Center for the Study of Writing at Carnegie Mellon University. Also, Benedict wrote Center for Learning curriculum units on *The Red Badge of Courage, A Portrait of the Artist as a Young Man, and Dandelion Wine.*

**The Publishing Team**

Rose Schaffer, M.A., President/Chief Executive Officer
Bernadette Vetter, M.A., Vice President
Diane Podnar, M.S., Managing Editor
Amy Richards, M.A., Editor


**Cover Design**

Mary Souders

List of credits found on Acknowledgments
page beginning on 92.

ISBN 1-56077-125-9

# Contents

# Introduction

*The Scarlet Letter* is a complex novel. Readers have to contend with the intrusion of the narrator commenting on the characters and their actions. Another difficulty lies in Hawthorne's language and style. Several exercises allow students to explore Hawthorne's writing and to try writing like him. This experience helps them to see the relationship between the writer and reader.

Since there are more than 130 years between Hawthorne's writing this novel and their reading of it, students will need to assess changing values toward the central issues of the novel. Hopefully, they will come to understand the universality of some of the issues. You might lead a class discussion about the unequal treatment of males and females caught in the same web. Also good discussion material is the fact that Hester is a strong female, emerging from her "punishment" with her integrity and personhood intact, even strengthened.

The development of the lessons and handouts in this unit has been guided by several underlying assumptions. Students are asked to write several pieces that try to replicate the experience of writers such as Stephen Crane. The rationale is drawn from research promulgated by such writers as Miles Myers, James Moffett, and others. By trying to write what they are to read, students can become more aware of the difficulty all writers encounter. They are asked to write to audiences other than just the teacher. Thus, they will be able to make certain rhetorical choices that will enhance their writing and their understanding that writing is not done in a vacuum.

Another underlying assumption upon which some of the lessons are built is found in the reader responses' theory of literary criticism promulgated by Wolfgang Iser and others. Students are shown that meaning is a negotiation between the reader and the text and that meaning evolves from this negotiation. This is not to say, however, that meaning is whatever the reader wants it to be. It does mean that the reader brings to the text his or her own experience and background as a necessary tool of understanding. Students, with your guidance, should see that every time they read or re-read a work, they bring new meaning to the text. Predicting the outcome of the novel or re-writing the ending are examples of negotiating with the text. Words and sentences within a text do not exist in isolation but lead the reader to "predict" the next word or next sentence. The same applies to ideas which also force students to become more careful readers of the text.

The lessons in this resource unit do not cover the full range of discussion or angles of approach possible for this novel. They are supplementary to any approaches you may have developed. You, the classroom teacher, know your class best and what will or will not work. You have the liberty to expand upon or alter any exercise in order to accomplish your goals and objectives.

# Preliminary Notes to the Teacher

The lessons and the handouts for *The Scarlet Letter* are designed to lead students inductively to some of the literary concepts that are relevant not only to this novel, but also to all works of fiction. With your guidance, they will come to understand the complexities of the novel's central characters and the point of view.

The lessons in this packet are designed to be sequential, with one lesson building on another. However, with preparation, the lessons may be used independently of sequence. Although each lesson is planned for a forty-five minute class segment, this may vary depending on the nature of the class or the discussions that are generated from the lessons. Two lessons are long term which is explained in Lesson 3.

One of the goals of the lessons in this packet is the development of a sense of scholarship among students beginning to visualize themselves as a community of scholars exploring a common topic from several angles. Students are encouraged to share findings as well as ideas with their classmates. The final paper outlined in Lesson 3 and brought to a close in Lesson 9 can be a symposium, a "celebration" of ideas (and maybe even a celebration of relief that they are finished with the novel).

One approach that you might wish to consider is the use of a reading journal. Ask students to write their reactions to each chapter. You can then use these entries as a basis for class discussion. Also, students can use the journals to summarize class discussions. You can then ascertain what they consider important in class discussions.

While there are several chapter checks in Lesson 10, you can also use the suggested writings to evaluate comprehension. Some of the writing assignments are designed so that students "translate" the work they are doing with the handouts into their own writing. From such assignments, you will be able to see what carry-over is being accomplished.

# Lesson 1

## Gathering Background Information: Pre-Reading Activity

## Objectives

- To understand Hawthorne's background against which the novel was written
- To understand the Puritan Age in which the story was set
- To discover how concepts and attitudes change

## Notes to the Teacher

This lesson is designed to develop a background against which to discuss the novel. Since it was written in a time period different from the actual time setting, students need to be aware of the difference in attitudes between these two time periods. They also will recognize a change of attitude from Hawthorne's time to their own. Investigating these differing attitudes will provide a firmer base for discussing some of the issues of the novel.

Before the actual reading assignments, you might want to allow several days for library research, class preparation for presentations, and for the presentations.

Four areas of investigation allow students to explore changing attitudes within the framework of research teams to encourage sense of scholarship and sharing of ideas. You might further refine the group investigation by assigning specific tasks to individuals within each group. In this way, everyone in a group shares responsibility for the entire project. Students then create ways to present material so that everyone understands the background material. Students should take notes on each group's presentation. Use of an evaluation procedure at the end of the presentations will insure attentive listening. This could take the form of a quiz covering the total material presented.

## Procedure

1. Distribute **Handout 1** and make group assignments, giving each group one of the areas of investigation. (Note: You may want each group to have a heterogeneous composite of strong and weaker students to ensure a collaborative learning atmosphere during the research.) Schedule time for reference work. Also, allow time for any interviews suggested for Investigation Three. After the research is completed, students are ready to prepare their presentations creatively in the form of short skits, reports complete with audio-visual aids, etc. Groups should be encouraged to prepare a handout sheet for the rest of the class. This sheet should summarize the most important facts. In this way, all members of the class will have a copy from which to study. Answers will vary.

2. **Handout 2** is designed to be done following the reports, with special concentration of Investigation One. Distribute **Handout 2** and have students work in their assigned groups. During the group process, each member should contribute at least five ideas. Answers will vary. This will ensure complete participation in the discussion. Allow as much time as necessary for a finished group paper that can be distributed to all members of the class as another resource.

   Structuring a Group Paper. In order to facilitate group contribution to the shaping of a paper, consider the following task structure.

   Primary Writer. This person takes the ideas listed by the Recorder and shapes them into a written product. The Primary Writer also provides each member of the group with a written draft of the paper.

   Recorder: This person lists and ranks the ideas contributed by each member of the group and gives them to the Primary Writer to shape into a paper.

   Checker: This person ensures that all members agree on the ideas presented and understand the reasons for them.

   Timer/Gatekeeper: This person keeps the group on target with relevant discussion within whatever time limitations are imposed.

After the Primary Writer has written the final draft, each member of the group must proofread and edit it. This will ensure that all agree with the form and substance of the final document. All members should sign the final draft to show that they have reached consensus. For evaluation purposes, you can assign a single grade to the final product with each member of the group receiving the same grade. This, again, ensures that every member contributes to the discussion. (Note: *Circles of Learning* by David Johnson, *et. al.*, Interaction Book Company, 7208 Cornelia Drive, Edina, MN 55435, 1986, is a good source for other types of collaborative group work.) This type of structure would work well for any type of group work.

Name _____

Date _____

# Investigative Reporting

## Directions

Investigate the area of study assigned to you. Then share this information with class members who also need it.

Investigation One

The action of *The Scarlet Letter* takes place in 1645. Investigate the Puritan Age to discover how the Puritans viewed the world. How did the Puritans define the following: guilt, sin, crime, adultery? What characterized Puritan religion and government?

Investigation Two

Hawthorne published *The Scarlet Letter* in 1850. Find out what the world was like at that time. How did the people of Hawthorne's time feel about guilt, sin, crime, adultery? Did Hawthorne believe the same way as his contemporaries? What were the major thoughts about religion at this time?

Investigation Three

Connotations of terms and ideas change over time. The action of *The Scarlet Letter* takes place in the 17th century. Hawthorne wrote the novel in the 19th century. You are reading it in the 20th century. Obviously, there have been many changes in attitudes during each period of time. How does today's society respond to the following: guilt, sin, crime, adultery? You might draw on television shows such as soap operas and on governmental and religious arenas. You might also consider conducting interviews with fellow students, ministers, adults, etc.

Investigation Four

The following terms are necessary for understanding certain concepts in *The Scarlet Letter*. While a dictionary definition might suffice in some cases, you may want to interview ministers, priests, and/or rabbis to get a fuller understanding of these terms in the context of religious teachings since the novel is intricately involved with the religious teachings of the Puritans. The terms are repentance, preternatural, remorse, contrition, penance, atonement, sorrow, penitence, revenge, sin.

**Directions**

After completing your initial investigation, prepare your findings to present to the class. Be as creative as possible. Whatever form your presentation takes, you are responsible for conveying accurate information.

Investigation Area _____

1. What are the important facts we learned during our investigation? (List the important facts.)

2. Based on our investigation, what did we learn about the attitudes of the time period we researched?

3. What do we want the rest of the class to know when we are finished with our presentation?

4. What is the best way to present this material to the rest of the class so that everyone will understand what we learned?

Name _____

Date _____

Synopsis of Material

## Directions
On this sheet you are to prepare a narrative synopsis of your findings and distribute copies of it to the rest of the class after your formal presentation.

Investigation Area _____

Name _____

Date _____

# Another Time, Another Place

**Directions**

You have just listened to several reports, including one based on the Puritan Age in which *The Scarlet Letter* took place. This setting is as removed from us as our time is from the Puritans. Working in your group, you are to write a description of what you think living during that time would have been like. Remember, many of the things that you take for granted were not available or even conceived during that time.

(Note: Your teacher will give you instructions for the writing of this group paper.)

Questions for Consideration

1.  What would it be like to live during the Puritan Age?

2.  How would you entertain yourself ?

3.  What hardships would you face?

4.  What would you not have to rely on?

5.  What would your attitudes be like?

# Lesson 2
## Exploring Hawthorne's Style of Writing: Another Pre-Reading Activity

## Objective

- To examine Hawthorne's style of writing

## Notes to the Teacher

Needless to say, Hawthorne's language and writing style are difficult for most readers. One of the handouts in this lesson asks the students to rewrite a passage from the novel as a means of "translating" Hawthorne. The exercise can be further implemented by selecting other passages for similar rewrites. Such effort can lead to a profitable class discussion on the use of language, especially as it reflects the mind of the author and of the audience. The other exercise involves the student in trying to duplicate Hawthorne's writing style. Students may be better prepared for the complexities of *The Scarlet Letter* if they complete these two handouts. Furthermore, they will gain an understanding of the relationship between a writer and an audience which will serve them well for the work with Point of View in Lesson 5.

## Procedure

1. Distribute **Handout 3**. Ask students to try to rewrite the passage from *The Scarlet Letter*. Encourage them to use simple sentences in order to contrast their writing and Hawthorne's.

**Suggested Responses** Part II
1. *Answers will vary.*
2. *Some responses might focus on the complexity of the language. Other responses might notice the lack of original tone in the language.*
3. *Hopefully, students will notice the intellectual quality of his writing, his craftsmanship.*
4. *Students should appreciate that the audience was familiar with the craft of writing as developed by Hawthorne and that many were at least as learned as the writer.*
5. *Today's readers are not accustomed to complex sentence structures and vocabulary. We use fewer complex sentences and "lighter" vocabulary words.*

2. Distribute **Handout 4**. Ask students to try to write like Hawthorne. Encourage them to duplicate the sentence structure, if not the vocabulary.

**Suggested Responses**

*Answers to questions 1–4 will vary. You might want the class to discuss the use and structure of language as a means of conveying ideas and as a reflection of the mind of the writer.*

Name _____

Date _____

# Rewriting Hawthorne

## Part I

### Directions

Read the following passage in the left column. In the right column, rewrite the passage as it might be written today.

Hawthorne's Passage

My Rewrite

The young minister, on ceasing to speak, had withdrawn a few steps from the group and stood partially concealed in the heavy folds of the window curtain, while the shadow of his figure, which the sunlight cast upon the floor, was tremulous with the vehemence of his appeal. Pearl, that wild and flighty little elf, stole softly towards him, and taking his hand in the grasp of both of her own, laid her cheek against it; a caress so tender, and withal so obtrusive, that her mother, who was looking on, asked herself, "Is that my Pearl?" Yet she knew that there was love in the child's heart, although it mostly revealed itself in passion, and hardly twice in her lifetime had been softened by such gentleness as now.

The minister—for, save the long-sought regards of woman, nothing is sweeter than these marks of childish preference, accorded spontaneously by a spiritual instinct, and therefore seeming to imply in us something truly worthy to be loved—the minister looked round, laid his hand on the child's head, hesitated for an instant, and then kissed her brow. Little Pearl's unwanted mood of sentiment lasted no longer; she laughed, and went capering down the hall, so airily, that old Mr. Wilson raised a question whether even her tiptoes touched the floor.[1]

[1]Nathaniel Hawthorne, *The Scarlet Letter* (Logan, Iowa: The Perfection Form Company, 1979), 115.

Part II

**Directions**

After completing the rewrite, answer the following questions.

1. What words did you have to look up in the dictionary?

2. What is lacking in your rewrite that is contained in the original?

3. What does your work with this passage show you about Hawthorne as a writer?

4. Assuming that a writer writes with an audience in mind or that a writer's audience understands a writer's style, what does this passage tell you about readers of Hawthorne's time?

5. What does it tell you about modern readers of Hawthorne?

Name _____

Date _____

# Writing Like the Author

## Directions

Try writing like Hawthorne using the same type of sentence structure and vocabulary. Respond to the questions that follow.

| Selected Passage | Rewrite A la Hawthorne |
|---|---|

### Selected Passage

"What Started Walking Home From School"

One spring day the boys stopped on their way home from school to drink from a puddle along the road. They used sheets from their spelling workbooks to make paper cups.

Except One.

He knelt down and drank straight from the puddle. This way he could see his face as he drank.

The others looked into their paper cups before they drank. This way they could see if there were any snakes in the water.

The one who drank kneeling down swallowed a snake. He saw its tail in the water between his eyes, but it was too late. The head was already down his throat.

When he stood up, the boys with paper cups said, "You swallowed a snake, didn't you?"

The other boys teased him and said his eyes looked different. The boy who swallowed the snake knelt down again and looked into the puddle. He saw a snake. Maybe it was another snake. Maybe it was the snake he had swallowed. He told the other boys he did not look different.

As they walked home, the boy felt the snake curl up in his stomach and go to sleep. This will be easy, he thought.

For supper, he said he was not hungry. He drank one glass of warm milk. The snake woke up and drank the warm milk, then fell asleep again.

When the boy went to bed, he saw that his stomach was bigger. So he slept on his back with his hands over his stomach to keep the snake warm. That night his dreams were different from anyone's.

The next day no one asked him about the snake.[2]

---

[2]Jim Heynen, *The Man Who Kept Cigars in His Cap*, (St. Paul, MN: Graywolf Press, 1979), 29.

Name _____

Date _____

1. What did your attempt to write like Hawthorne show you about your own writing?

2. What did it show about Hawthorne's writing?

3. Which is easier, "translating" Hawthorne or trying to write like Hawthorne?

4. Why?

# Lesson 3
## The Beginning—Symbols and Character: Chapters 1–6

## Objectives

- To enter the world of the *The Scarlet Letter*
- To explore the use of some conventional and some non-clichéd symbols used in the novel
- To begin character study

## Notes to the Teacher

This lesson, including Chapter 1–6, is divided into several parts, each requiring that students work in assigned groups that will function occasionally throughout the reading of the novel. This assignment calls for each group to present a final report of their work.

Since there are many sources in which to examine some of the more conventional symbols in *The Scarlet Letter*, this lesson allows students to explore some non-clichéd symbols and thus develop an understanding of how symbols make meaning and how meaning makes symbols. The reading from Roland Bartel assists in thinking through the discovery of symbols. The reading from Paul Tillich also will help students expand their understanding of symbology.

The handout on character study is an inductive approach in which conclusions about the characters are drawn by looking at their significant actions and statements. Formulating conclusions about the characters requires students to read the text closely, thus verifying that they are fulfilling reading assignments.

## Procedure

1. Distribute **Handout 5.** Ask students to read the statement from Roland Bartel's book and answer the questions that follow. Answers will vary based on experience with symbols. After completing question 5, a class discussion on the different criteria that have evolved will lead to consensus that best suits study of *The Scarlet Letter*. This ensures that the students are all working from a common base.

**Suggested Responses**

1. *Answers will vary depending on students' background. Brainstorming upon completing this question will give a fuller picture of their understanding.*
2. *Responses will vary, but the common sense approach to discovering symbols can be emphasized.*
3. *Answers may point to extensive study of those items throughout the entire work. Some students may mention the need to be alert to the context of a symbol within a work.*
4. *Students should see that a symbol is a symbol, but we should avoid playing "symbol-hunters," seeing a symbol at every turn of the page.*
5. *Again answers will vary, but some criteria should include: (a) the repetition of an object; (b) its reference to meanings outside the work; (c) cautious observation.*

2. **Handout 6** is an optional assignment for the most capable students. This can be a homework assignment. Question 5 will generate class discussion. Answers will vary in accordance with students' backgrounds and interests.

3. Distribute **Handout 7.** You may select from the list of symbols which follows or use some of your own choice. A mix of conventional and non-cliché symbols usually is associated with *The Scarlet Letter.* The non-clichéd symbols are more universal in nature and are drawn from such people as Joseph Campbell and Mircea Eliade. They are not usually explored in the study of this novel. You might consider assigning the non-clichéd symbols to the more experienced readers. This is a long term project culminating in Lesson 10 in which all students will have an opportunity to explain their work with symbols.

If students work in small groups of two or three, a wider range of symbolism can be explored. Most of this work can be done as homework with occasional class time set aside for group partners to compare notes.

| Non-Cliched Symbols | Conventional Symbols |
| --- | --- |
| Trees | Scaffolding |
| Thresholds/doors | Gold |
| Water | Colors |
| Windows/mirrors | Darkness/Light |
| Steps | Vegetation |
| Triads | Rosebush |
| Moon/Sun | Letter "A" |
| Drapery/Curtains | Night/Day |
| Reflections | Forest |

(Note: You might want to explain why symbols of Column 1 are not cliched symbols in the context of *The Scarlet Letter.*)

4. Distribute **Handout 8** and assign appropriate groups. This long-term assignment is to be done over the entire reading of the novel.

## Optional Activities

Consider assigning **Handout 5** to some groups and **Handout 6** to alternate groups within the class. Some students can work on symbolism, others on character. Small groups can become "experts" in a specific field of study, and can be held responsible for "teaching" the rest of the class about their area of concentrated study.

Students can begin writing "themes" by doing one or both of the following which are "soup starters" for major themes and can be developed over the course of studying the novel. Whenever a paper is warranted, students can then pull out these "starters" and develop them into a major paper.

1. Self-Generated Questions. Van Nostrand, Knoblauch, and Pettigrew, *The Process of Writing,* (Houghton Mifflin, 1982) propose that "self-generated questions" help a writer "create" a reader and thus clarify meaning. These same questions can also be used by readers as they approach a text. Ask the writer these types of questions:
   a. Who is telling me this and on what authority?
   b. What is the significance of what you are telling me?
   c. How will it affect me?
   d. What are the consequences of what you are telling me?
   e. Why should I pay attention to it?
   f. Are you telling me everything I ought to know or want to know?

   This is a way to encourage a reader to enter into a dialogue with the text and its author. After you suggest such questions, let the students ask the author their own questions about the text and, if they can, answer them. You can ask students to respond to these questions after each chapter or groups of chapters. They can write their answers in a reading journal.

2. Microthemes. Although this, like self-generated questions, is a technique employed in planning one's writing, it can be adapted to reading and writing about a text. Microthemes are skeletal plans which enable students to demonstrate their understanding of different kinds of writing tasks. The authors, John Bean, Dean Drenk and F. D. Lee, suggest four different kinds of microthemes:
   a. Summary-writing
   b. Thesis-support
   c. Data-provided
   d. Quandary-posing

   The microthemes are written in outline on 3x5 index cards. You can give the students a thesis to be demonstrated, facts or data that need a thesis to organize them, a question that has to be answered, etc. Then send the students to the text and let them root. Microthemes can be written throughout the study of the novel. You can design each one to be part of a longer paper which evenutally you will expect students to write. The index cards could be collected and returned when students are ready to write the longer paper.

Name _____

Date _____

# What Does a Symbol Mean?

## Directions

After you read the following excerpt about symbols, please join the group to which you have been assigned to discuss the questions that follow the reading.

> Learning to recognize symbols is largely a matter of using our intuition and our background in literature. We should remember first of all that anything may be a symbol, that a symbol is any sign that has acquired extra meaning. It may be an object, a gesture, an incident, a person, a plot, a color, a sound, a pattern or sequence of action—anything that reminds us of something else that in turn seems applicable to the text before us. The word *may* is crucial. Although we must develop a sensitivity to the possibility that anything unusual may be symbolic, we must refrain from concluding that everything unusual is symbolic. A balance between sensitivity to the possibility of symbols and a common sense approach to the basic meaning of the text is the best guide.[1]

1. What do you already know about symbols in general?

2. How does Bartel's explanation add to that understanding?

3. After reading the above, what should you do in order to determine whether or not some thing, some person, some action, etc. might be symbolically used in a work of fiction?

[1]Roland Bartel, "Metaphors and Symbols: Forays into Language," (NCTE Journal, 1983), 62.

4. Explain what Bartel means by saying: "The word *may* is crucial. Although we must develop a sensitivity to the possibility that anything unusual *may* be symbolic, we must refrain from concluding that everything ususual *is* symbolic.
   How can this best be done?

5. Based on this reading, draw up a list of criteria that you will use as a guide to determine what the symbols are in *The Scarlet Letter*." (Note: Be sure to keep a copy of this list since you will need it later.)

Name _____

Date _____

# Another View of Symbolism

## Directions

Read the following characteristics of a symbol in relation to the work you did in **Handout 5** and answer the ensuing questions.

1. A symbol points beyond itself to something else. Some signs are called symbols which cause some confusion. Signs can be replaced while symbols cannot.

2. A symbol participates in that to which it points. The flag participates in the power and dignity of the nation for which it stands.

3. A symbol opens levels of reality which otherwise are closed for us. All arts create symbols for a level of reality which cannot be reached in any other way, not even scientifically.

4. A symbol unlocks dimensions and elements of our souls which correspond to the dimensions and elements of reality. A great play gives us not only a new vision of the human scene, but it opens up hidden depths of our own being.

5. A symbol cannot be produced intentionally. Symbols grow out of the individual or collective unconscious and cannot function without being accepted by the unconscious dimension of our being.

6. A symbol grows when the situation is ripe for it and dies when the situation changes. This is a consequence of the fact that symbols cannot be invented.

Genuine symbols are created in every sphere of man's cultural creativity.
Source: Adaptation: Paul Tillich, *Dynamics of Faith,* (Harper and Row, 1957) pp. 41–43.

Name _____

Date _____

1. How do these statements increase your understanding of what a symbol is?

2. What statements do you agree with? Why?

3. What statements do you disagree with? Why?

4. In what way do these statements compare with those of Bartel in **Handout 5?**

5. Select a symbol used in a literary work previously studied. Examine it in light of both Bartel's and Tillich's statements.

Name _____

Date _____

# Symbols Chart

## Directions

Use the following chart in your study of symbols in *The Scarlet Letter*. Ask your teacher for additional copies if needed. Keep your own log of symbols as you read. Work on the chart in the group to which you were assigned for work on **Handout 1.**

Each group will be assigned a specific symbol to study throughout the novel. After reading the novel, each group will make a presentation based on the work done.

| Chapter | Page | Description | Significance |
|---------|------|-------------|--------------|
|         |      |             |              |

Name _____

Date _____

# Character Study

## Directions

Keep the following log on the character assigned to your group. In addition, keep your own log over the entire reading of the novel. Get additional forms from your teacher as you need them.

| Chapter/Page: | |
|---|---|
| **Significant Action:** | |
| **Significant Statement:** | |
| **Insight into Character Provided by Action and Statement** | |
| **Personal Reaction to Character** | |

# Lesson 4

## The Artist in Residence: Chapters 7–12

### Objective

- To understand the dynamics of visual art
- To view a written passage with the same understanding applied to visual art
- To scrutinize the character of Roger Chillingworth

### Notes to the Teacher

This lesson asks students to do some interdisciplinary study and divergent thinking by looking at a work of art and transferring their conclusions to the written art. Rembrandt was chosen as the artist because of the tonal qualities of his work and the application of contrasts between light and dark. His work evokes some of the same somberness found in Hawthorne's "painting," making a good transitional element for discussion.

After students have studied the painting and a selected descriptive scene from the novel, they can then look more intensively at a character in the novel. This microscopic look will apply the same techniques as a method of understanding how a character is drawn in order to convey a mood or timbre of being.

### Procedure

1. Distribute **Handout 9.** An art teacher can be invited to explain the terms listed in the handout. The art teacher could also lead a discussion about the Rembrandt paintings chosen for this lesson because they convey some of the same tonal qualities as *The Scarlet Letter.* Suggested paintings include *The Night Watch* or various self-portraits.

   **Suggested Responses**
   1. *The light focuses on certain areas of the painting to accentuate either people or objects.*
   2. *After looking at the highlights, the viewer attempts to see what is concealed in the darkness.*
   3. *Answers will vary, but students should note the somberness of the overall painting.*
   4. *The light comes from outside the painting. This allows the viewer to think about the reason for the lighting and why certain areas are highlighted and others are not.*

2. Distribute **Handout 10** and allow students time to collaborate on answering the questions. Part I answers will vary, but discussion will pull together any loose ends.

   **Suggested Responses** Part II
   1. *Students should note any words or phrases that indicate the light/dark, somber quality of the scene. For example, ". . . the mystery of the primeval forest."*
   2. *Answers will vary.*
   3. *Feelings might include oppression, mystery, foreboding, depending on word and phrase choices.*
   4. *Hawthorne creates a sense of coldness and isolation by describing how the sunlight keeps moving away. Rembrandt also isolates with his use of light and dark tones.*

3. Distribute **Handout 11.** This handout is designed to allow students to examine a character in the same manner as they did the Rembrandt painting and the scene from the novel.

   **Suggested Responses**
   1. *Answers will vary.*
   2. *Answers will vary.*
   3. *There is the same use of lght and dark contrasts and pictorial descriptions. Some students might notice that the quality of light references are different.*
   4. *Contrasts include his dark qualities being emphasized by the references to light and fire.*

5. *The tone is one of evil and cunning.*
6. *Answers may vary but should focus on the evil intentions of the coldness of his character which conflict with his profession.*

4. Distribute **Handout 12.** This handout is designed as a journal writing outside class.

### Suggested Responses

1. *Students should recognize the "brush strokes" of Hawthorne's writing. The descriptions are pictorial in nature and would be easy to draw.*
2. *Answers may vary but should mention the pictorial, effective nature of these descriptions.*
3. *Students should be able to discern the somber, highlighting qualities.*

## Optional Activities

In connection with the study of the Rembrandt paintings, you might obtain *Art & Man* magazine published by Scholastic. The September/ October, 1983 edition (Vol. 14, No. 1) focuses on Rembrandt. You might also order a six-minute film entitled *Rembrandt* (catalog number 117) from the free-loan extension program of National Gallery of Art. (Address: The Extension Program, National Gallery of Art, Washington, D.C., 20565). This film focuses on Rembrandt's dramatic use of color in some of his most famous paintings and prints.

Name _____

Date _____

# Rembrandt the Painter

**Directions**

The following terms are associated with painting. As you observe the selected paintings, notice how these terms are used in describing the paintings. Formulate definitions for these terms as they apply to art. Also consider and discuss the questions about technique and effect.

1. Nuance

2. Chiaroscuro

3. Hue

4. Tint

5. Contrast

6. Value

7. Shading

**Directions**

As you study the picture, consider the following questions.

1. How does Rembrandt use lighting to draw your attention to various people or objects in the painting?

2. How does he use darkness to accentuate other aspects of the painting?

3. What is the overall impression you get about the tonal quality of the painting from the colors and light and dark mixtures of the painting?

4. Does the light come from a source within or outside the painting? How does this affect your perception of the painting?

# Hawthorne the Painter

## Part I

### Directions
After completing the study of Rembrandt's paintings in **Handout 9,** read the passage below from *The Scarlet Letter* and answer the questions that follow.

> The road, after the two wayfarers had crossed from the peninsula to the mainland, was no other than a footpath. It straggled onward into the mystery of the primeval forest. This hemmed it in so narrowly, and stood so black and dense on either side, and disclosed such imperfect glimpses of the sky above, that, to Hester's mind, it imagined not amiss the moral wilderness in which she had so long been wandering. The day was chill and somber. Overhead was a gray expanse of cloud, slightly stirred, however, by a breeze, so that a gleam of the flickering sunshine might now and then be seen at its solitary play along the path. This flitting cheerfulness was always at the further extremity of some long vista through the forest. The sportive sunlight—feebly sportive, at best, in the predominant pensiveness of the day and scene—withdrew itself as they came nigh, and left the spots where it had danced the drearier, because they had hoped to find them bright.[1]

1. Underline any words or phrases that suggest the tonal qualities you found in the Rembrandt painting.

2. Draw circles around any words or phrases that correspond with the art terms on **Handout 9.**

3. What musical instrument best describes this scene? _____

4. What cloth or material best describes this scene? _____

5. What one sound best describes this scene? _____

[1]Hawthorne, *The Scarlet Letter,* 175.

Part II

**Questions**

1. How does Hawthorne paint this scene using words instead of paint?

2. How do the questions of **Handout 9** help you to visualize this scene?

3. What feeling does Hawthorne evoke in you as you read this scene? How does he accomplish this?

4. How does he use contrast of light and dark in this scene? How is this similar to Rembrandt's use of light and dark?

Name _____

Date _____

# The Painting of a Soul

## Directions

Read the descriptions of Roger Chillingworth. As you read these passages, think of the work you did with the Rembrandt painting and the scene from the novel. Apply some of the same techniques in analyzing Chillingworth's character.

### Passage 1

Sometimes, a light glimmered out of the physician's eyes, burning blue and ominous, like the reflection of a furnace, or let us say, like one of those gleams of ghastly fire that darted from Bunyan's awful doorway in the hillside and quivered on the pilgrim's face. The soil where this dark miner was working had perchance shown indications that encouraged him.

### Passage 2

Then, after long search into the minister's dim interior, and turning over many precious materials in the shape of high aspirations for the welfare of his race, warm love of souls, pure sentiments, natural piety, strengthened thought and study, and illuminated by revelation—all of which invaluable gold was perhaps no better than rubbish to the seeker—he would turn back, discouraged, and begin his quest towards another point. He groped along as stealthily, with as cautious a tread, and as wary an outlook, as a thief entering a chamber where a man lies only half-asleep—or, it may be, broad awake—with purpose to steal the very treasure which this man guards as the apple of his eye. In spite of his premeditated carefulness, the floor would now and then creak; his garments would rustle; the shadow of his presence, in a forbidden proximity, would be thrown across his victim.

### Passage 3

But, with a wild look of wonder, joy, and horror! With what a ghastly rapture, as it were, too mighty to be expressed only by the eye and features, and therefore bursting forth through the whole ugliness of his figure, and making itself even riotously manifest by the extravagant gestures with which he threw up his arms towards the ceiling, and stamped his foot upon the floor! Had a man seen old Roger Chillingworth, at that moment of his ecstasy, he would have had no need to ask how Satan comports himself when a precious human soul is lost to heaven and won into his kingdom.[2]

[2]Ibid, 127, 128, 135–136.

Name _____

Date _____

Obviously, the way a writer describes a person is different from the way he or she would describe a scene. But in both cases, the author's "brush strokes of color" are words. Answer the following questions about the preceding passages.

1. What mineral would best describe Chillingworth in the above passages?

2. What sound would best describe him?

3. How is Hawthorne's description of Chillingworth similar to his description in the scene on **Handout 10**?

4. What contrasts, either direct or indirect, does Hawthorne use in his description of Chillingworth in these passages?

5. What is the overall tone of these descriptions?

6. What insight into Chillingworth's character do the contrasts and tone of the descriptions provide?

Name _____

Date _____

# Viewing the Painting

**Directions**

Viewing a painting is a visual experience. In one sense so is reading literature since you must use your eyes. The significant difference between a painting and a novel is that the artist uses paints to represent a scene and a novelist uses words. The reader must supply the visual aspect of the novel by means of imagination. Symbolism and characterization are "brush strokes" of a novelist's palette. Refer to the handouts in Lesson 3 and Lesson 4, and respond to the following questions in your journal or through class discussion.

1.  How has Hawthorne used words and symbols to create a picture?

2.  What do the descriptions both of the scene in **Handout 10** and of Roger Chillingworth in **Handout 11** tell you about Hawthorne as a "painter" of verbal pictures?

3.  How are Rembrandt and Hawthorne similar in their use of color, light and dark, and contrast?

# Lesson 5

## Point of View—Intimacy between Reader and Narrator: Chapters 13—19

## Objectives

- To understand point of view as a concept
- To apply understanding of point of view to a literary work
- To demonstrate the relationship between a narrator and a reader as a function of point of view

## Notes to the Teacher

Point of view in a story is sometimes a very difficult concept for students to grasp, especially in its importance to understanding the story. Students have an easy time of visualizing a point of view as demonstrated in a painting, photograph, or movie. By capitalizing on this skill, we can move to understanding point of view in a piece of writing.

The next step is for students to recognize the choices a writer makes when adopting a point of view. Students will then be able to understand that the readers' reactions to the story and characters are shaped and colored by the narrator's point of view. The exercises in this lesson will help students understand point of view and apply knowledge to the story.

1. Distribute **Handout 13.** Ask students to study the picture then answer the questions.

   **Suggested Responses**
   1. *In front of the subject, on the scaffold*
   2. *It shows Hester climbing the stairs and that she is more important than the people around her.*
   3. *The artist wants the student to see Hester's strength, possibly her determination and separation from the crowd. Hester is the center of attention, the focus of the picture.*
   4. *The scarlet letter, Pearl, the scaffold*
   5. *The artist is sympathetic to Hester's plight.*

2. Distribute **Handout 14.** The chart is comprehensive but may need some explanation. Some terms may be unfamiliar for aspects of point of view that students already know. They differ from more familiar terms like "first person limited," or "omniscient." The discussion will provide a good basis to explore the relationship between the narrator and the reader, between the point of view and the story.

   **Suggested Responses**
   1. *Students should see that point of view is very important. A restatement of the function of point of view in their own words would be appropriate.*
   2. *Students should see that there is essentially no difference. Both present a view of the world through certain colorations and hues.*
   3. *Students should see that a point of view helps to define a structure for the story and that meaning is shaped or defined by point of view. By examining what a narrator presents and the way in which it is presented, a reader can begin to realize the themes of a story.*
   4. *Dramatic structure is the physical structure of a story, the narrative framework.*

3. Distribute **Handout 15.** This handout shuttles students between thinking about the novel and thinking about their own experiences. By identifying the point of view of the novel, students can begin to understand what Hawthorne is doing through his narrator. Students are then asked to examine their own experiences from their own points of view. By asking them to retell those experiences from another point of view, they can be led into a discussion of changes and choices necessitated by different points of view.

**Suggested Responses**

1. *Students may have a difficult time with this since there is the fact of the author's intrusion into the novel. Basically, the point of view is a privileged narrator with moments of the dramatized point of view. Some students might question the reliability of this narrator. Others might feel offended by the commentary that seems to moralize about the actions and thoughts of the characters.*

2. *Students should select passages that show the narrator's ability to enter the minds of the characters while interplaying both long summaries and character dialogue with authorial commentary.*

3. *Answers will vary.*

4. *Anwers will vary.*

5. *Descriptions will vary.*

6. *Some of the responses should indicate an understanding of size relationship. A four-year-old child would not be able to see certain things and would need to be lifted. Another factor to look for is the language that would be used by a four-year-old child.*

4. Distribute **Handout 16.** This handout asks students to move from a global comprehension of point of view and apply understanding to a particular character. Stress the relationship of the author/narrator to a character. How that character is shaped and presented is a function of point of view.

**Suggested Responses**

1. *He seems to be at her elbow.*

2. *There seems to be a tone of respect for her, especially in the fact that she appears to have overcome the situation instead of letting the situation overcome her. There also is a tone of awe and wonder at her accomplishments.*

3. *Answers will vary.*

4. *Answers will vary but students should notice the respect in Hawthorne's attitude toward Hester.*

5. *She has become stronger and moved herself into the "labyrinth of the mind."*

6. *Answers will vary depending on previous responses.*

## Optional Activities

One way to underscore the concept of point of view is to have students draw a picture from a particular point of view. They may select a scene from the novel and render it as a drawing with some of the tonal qualities of the scenes as described by Hawthorne.

Name _____

Date _____

# Point of View: Painting

**Directions**
An author's use of point of view lets the reader see things in a certain light or perspective. Look at this picture and answer the questions that follow.

1.  Where is the artist standing relative to the subject of the painting?

2.  What does this position tell about what is important in the painting? What is important to the artist?

3.  What does the artist want you to think about the subject? How do you know?

4.  What details does the artist seem to emphasize in this picture?

5.  What insight do these details give you into the mind of the artist?

Name _____

Date _____

# Point of View: Literature

## Directions

Look carefully at the following chart and try to understand what each point of view means.

### Points of View

|  | Outside Narrator | | Inside Narrator | |
|---|---|---|---|---|
|  | **Privileged** | **Effaced** | **Dramatized** | **Restricted** |
| **Identity in Story** | Not a character | Not a character | A character | Not a character |
| **Voice** | Third-person pronouns; may occasionally use first-person pronouns | Third-person pronouns | First-person pronouns | Third-person pronouns |
| **Access to Character's Consciousness** | Unlimited access to consciousness of all the characters | No access: does not enter consciousness of characters; reveals their thoughts and feelings through dialogue and action | Access to consciousness of one character—himself | Access to consciousness of one character or to consciousness of a "community" of characters through whose perceptions he conveys the story |
| **Presence** | Calls attention to himself as narrator through: 1. descriptions conveyed in his own voice and reflecting his position outside the events of the story; 2. narrative analysis or interpretation of character, incident, and setting; 3. adoption of perspectives different from his own when he reveals the thoughts of certain characters at close range. | Conveys almost no sense of his presence, since he generally gives no long description or narrative analysis and does not adopt different perspectives | Dominates story; relates his own experience or, as witness, someone else's | Speaks in his own voice but submerges his vision into the character(s) whose perspective(s) serve as narrative focus |
| **Reliability** | Generally reliable because he frequently stands close to the implied author | Reliable in that he is "neutral" | Frequently unreliable because his self-knowledge and knowledge of others is imperfect | Ranges from reliable to unreliable, depending on the character(s) whose consciousness(es) he reveals and on the presence or absence of "clues" affirming or negating implicit attitudes and values |

[1]Barbara McKenzie, ed., *The Process of Fiction* (Orlando, FL: Harcourt, Brace & World, Inc. 1969), 8–9.

## Directions

Read the following and answer the questions that follow. Refer to the chart as you are reading this passage.

The Function of Point of View

The fiction writer's chief structural resource is *point of view*—at its most fundamental level, the physical vantage point occupied by the narrator in a story or novel and the device by which the writer establishes the "authority" for his fiction. For the writer, point of view is the basic means of ordering and unifying his material. Once he has decided upon the position and, further, upon the disposition of his narrator (choices that are often partly unconscious), all other ingredients of the work must relate to his decision. For the reader, point of view, by affecting the shape of the story, determines how the story material reaches him and how he perceives the fictional events.

The narrator of a story stands in one of two basic relationships to the events of the story: outside or inside the action. The task of the critical reader is to ascertain the effects of each narrative perspective and disposition. In addition, he must concern himself with the matter of "open" and "closed" consciousness and their relation to point of view. An open consciousness is a character whose inner thoughts are revealed to the reader. Frequently, the author depicts setting or action through the perceptions of such a character. A closed consciousness is a character whose inner thoughts are hidden, making the reader view him through such externals as physical action, dialogue, the reaction of others, and personal appearance. Ultimately, the reader must see how point of view, as Mark Schorer contends, serves as a mode of thematic definition (as a way of conveying meaning), as well as a mode of dramatic definition (as a determiner of structure).[2]

[2]Ibid, 7, 8.

Name _____

Date _____

## Questions

1. How important is point of view to your understanding of any story? Explain.

2. What is the difference between an artist's use of point of view and a writer's use of point of view?

3. What is meant by "thematic definition"? How do you think point of view helps to discover a theme or themes of a story?

4. What is meant by "dramatic definition"? How might point of view help you discover the structure of a story?

# Hawthorne and Hester: Part I

**Directions**

From the chosen point of view, we learn **what** the author is thinking about a character, a scene or an action in the story. Re-read Chapter 13 of *The Scarlet Letter* carefully and answer the following questions.

Outside of Fiction

1. What is the point of view of this novel thus far? (Choose the appropriate one from the chart on **Handout 14.**)

2. How do you know this? Support your answer with direct proof from the novel.

3. In real life, we often interpret actions, events, and people based on our own point of view. We make judgments and decisions based on our experience as individuals. Recount here one important event from your own life.

4. Re-read your accounting. How did you present it? How would your best friend recount that event? What is the difference?

5. Write a description of a water fountain from the point of view of a four-year-old child.

6. What choices did you have to make in describing the water fountain as a four-year-old child would view it?

# Hawthorne and Hester: Part II

Inside of Fiction

In fiction, as readers we are always looking through someone else's eyes. This person, we call the narrator. The narrator is one who makes judgments about the characters and actions. The story is filtered through the narrator's eyes, and we make judgments about characters based on what the narrator tells us.

1. Where do you see the narrator standing in relationship to Hester in Chapter 13?

2. How does the narrator feel about Hester?

3. What specific words or phrases indicate this?

4. Look carefully at the following sentences and explain how they help to substantiate the narrator's attitudes and judgments about Hester in Chapter 13.

    a. The links that united her to the rest of human kind—links of flowers, or silk, or gold, or whatever the material—had all been broken.

    b. It was perceived, too, that while Hester never put forward even the humblest title to share in the world's privileges—further than to breathe the common air, and earn daily bread for little Pearl and herself by the faithful labor of her hands—she was quick to acknowledge her sisterhood with the race of man, whenever benefits were to be conferred.

    c. She was self-ordained a Sister of Mercy; or we may say, the world's heavy hand had so ordained her, when neither the world nor she looked forward to this result. The letter was the symbol of her calling. Such helpfulness was found in her—so much power to do and power to sympathize—that many people refused to interpret the scarlet "A" by its original signification. They said that it meant "Able"; so strong was Hester Pryne, with a woman's strength.

    d. She who was once a woman, and ceased to be so, might at any moment become a woman again, if there were only the magic touch to effect the transfiguration.

    e. Much of the marble coldness of Hester's impression was to be attributed to the circumstances that her life had turned, in a great moment, from passion and feeling to thought.

    f. Thus Hester Pryne, wandered without a clew in the dark labyrinth of the mind; now turned aside by an insurmountable precipice; now ghastly scenery all around her, and a home and comfort nowhere.[3]

[3]Hawthorne, *The Scarlet Letter*, 154–160.

Name _____

Date _____

5. What do these excerpts tell you about Hester?

6. In what ways is the presentation of Hester in Chapter 13 different from that of previous chapters?

# Lesson 6
## Setting—Landscaping the Story: Chapters 13–19

## Objectives

- To demonstrate the relationship between setting and point of view
- To observe how setting is a reflection of the characters' minds and thoughts
- To analyze setting and to see how setting can be an indicator of theme

## Notes to the Teacher

This lesson asks students to concentrate on one of the settings of the novel, namely the forest. The close reading of Chapters 13 through 19 will afford students a better understanding of Hawthorne's use of setting. While this lesson focuses on only one of the novel's settings, other settings can be selected for assignment.

## Procedures

1. Distribute **Handout 17.** Ask students to read the commentary about setting. They may work in groups to answer the first three questions. Question 4 should be done individually.

   **Suggested Responses**
   1. *Answers will vary but should focus on the interdependence of setting, character, and point of view.*
   2. *Answers should provide a recapitulation of the commentary.*
   3. *Again, this should be a recapitulation of the commentary.*
   4. *Answers will vary.*

2. Distribute **Handout 18.** This handout may be done as a homework assignment. Its purpose is for students to draw on their own experiences as a prelude to working with Hawthorne's descriptions of the forest. Emphasize the use of concrete and specific detail in the writing of the descriptions.

   **Suggested Responses**
   *Answers will vary.*

3. Distribute **Handout 19.** It may be used either as a group or an individual activity. Students will give an overall description of the forest in the first column of the chart. They will select a representative particular description to list under the second column. The third column asks for an overall mood of the chapter. Answers will vary in Part I.

   **Suggested Responses** Part II
   1. *Answers will vary, but students should notice the impassive quality of the forest.*
   2. *Hawthorne describes both the somberness in Chapters 16, 17, and 18 and the "flood of sunshine" in Chapter 19.*
   3. *Answer will vary, but focus should be on the use of nature in a romance.*
   4. *Answers will vary.*
   5. *Answers will vary.*

4. Distribute **Handout 20.** There are several options for student work on this handout. They might work in a one-group setting in which each member of the group is assigned a different character for Part I from Chapters 16 through 19. Each member is then responsible for sharing discoveries with the other members. Another group configuration might be preferred with the entire group working on one of the characters and each member contributing to the completion of **Handout 20.** If this option is used, a class discussion will afford an opportunity for oral presentations of each character.

39

**Suggested Responses** Part II

1. *Answers will vary depending on the assigned character.*
2. *Again, answers will vary depending on assigned character.*
3. *Answers will vary depending on assigned character.*
4. *Answers will vary depending on assigned character.*
5. *Students should see the reflection of the characters' moods in the physical description as well as the affective description of the forest. This is most evident in Chapter 19 when there is elation in the characters and a brightening of the forest by the sunlight.*
6. *Students should see that Hawthorne is playing with emotions in the characters and therefore making the reader more sympathetic toward their plights and sufferings.*
7. *Students might focus on literary associations rather than on personal associations. For example, the Garden of Eden, "Young Goodman Brown," "Sleeping Beauty," and "The Legend of Sleepy Hollow" all contain associative values with the forest.*
8. *Students should begin to see the association with evil and Satan, especially in the description of Dimmesdale as "The Black Man." This is also evident in "Young Goodman Brown."*
9. *Several themes are suggested, among them the use of nature in this novel.*

## Optional Activities

The activities in this lesson lend themselves to using either the self-generating questions or the microthemes mentioned in Lesson 3. Artistic students may enjoy drawing forest scenes, trying to capture the mood described by Hawthorne. Other students might create collages.

Name _____

Date _____

# Setting: Reflection of the Soul

## Directions

Please read the following commentary about the setting and answer the questions that follow.

The Importance of Setting

Setting is the representation in fiction of the time and place that constitute the environment of the action. Incorporating the tangible and spiritual aspects of physical locations and historical eras, setting includes the depiction of objects and institutions peculiar to certain places and periods.

Closely related to characterization, setting enhances the credibility of the characters by providing a visible context for them. It can also influence, sometimes even control their lives. As with character and plot, the establishment of setting calls for selectivity by the writer. Often, what he chooses not to describe is particularly significant, and frequently what is included alerts us to what is missing.

As the writer may depict a rich variety of characters, so he may set his story in any time or any place—actual or imaginary. He may invent a place and time, creating fanciful landscapes sustained only by his imagination and putting the action backward into a remote era or forward into a visionary future.

By setting his story in a "real" location or in one resembling an actual place, the writer releases a host of associations in the reader.

By establishing a "real" setting, the writer can manipulate the reader's knowledge in still another way. He can choose to confirm preconceptions about a particular place or to reverse those expectations.

Like any other aspect of fiction, setting is affected by point of view. In stories told by an effaced narrator, description of setting is customarily objective and brief, with the narrator providing only those details necessary to convey a minimal sense of place. In contrast, there are often copious descriptions in stories told by a privileged narrator, who is at liberty to depict setting either through his own perceptions or through those of his character.

Setting is related to mood as well as to point of view. Mood refers to the atmosphere that surrounds and helps to define the world in which the characters move. Thus, mood involves the feeling that emanates from certain locales or accrues from particular actions. Although intangible, mood can be an unshakeable quality that affects our responses to a story, as in real life we are affected by the atmosphere of certain places.[1]

[1] McKenzie, ed., *The Process of Fiction,* 29–32

1. Using your own words, describe the importance of setting.

2. How are character and setting related? Why is this important?

3. How are point of view and setting related? Why is this important?

4. Describe a "real life" place of your experience. Try to convey the mood of the place through your description. (Note: with this description, you should demonstrate your understanding of the description of setting.)

# Seeing the Forest for the Trees

**Directions**

In this handout you are to describe your experience and association with nature in general and the forest in particular. Respond to the following questions carefully. In writing your descriptions, be as graphic and as concrete as possible.

1.  Describe a scene in a forest that you remember most vividly from first-hand experience or from viewing a picture. Try to capture the texture of the trees, the forest floor, sounds, time of year, temperature, and lighting.

2.  How did your stay in the woods make you feel?

3.  How do you feel now in recalling this scene?

4.  What does the word "nature" mean to you? Why?

5.  How does your feeling about nature in general and the forest scene you described color your description? Was your experience a positive or negative one? How did this tinge your description?

# The Hawthorne Trees

Part I

## Directions

Re-read Chapters 16 through 19 carefully. Pay particular attention to the descriptions of the forest in each chapter. Describe the mood that each chapter presents through its description of the woods.

|  | Overall Description of Forest | Particular Description of Some Part of the Forest | Overall Mood Evoked by Description |
|---|---|---|---|
| Chapter 16 |  |  |  |
| Chapter 17 |  |  |  |
| Chapter 18 |  |  |  |
| Chapter 19 |  |  |  |

Name _____

Date _____

## Part II

1. What overall impression do you get about the forest based on your charting.

2. What differences do you see in the descriptions through the different chapters?

3. What impressions about nature does Hawthorne present with his descriptions of the forest in these chapters?

4. What associations about forests, trees, and nature do you bring to the text? (Base this answer on your work with **Handout 18.**)

5. How have these colored your reading of the chapters? How are they different from Hawthorne's impressions?

Name _____

Date _____

# Among the Trees

Part I

**Directions**

Note the characters' actions and feelings when they are in the forest. Concentrate on the character assigned to you.

|  | Overall Description of Forest | Particular Action of a Character in Forest | Feeling of Character in Forest |
|---|---|---|---|
| Chapter 16 |  |  |  |
| Chapter 17 |  |  |  |
| Chapter 18 |  |  |  |
| Chapter 19 |  |  |  |

Name _____

Date _____

## Part II

1.  What did you notice about your character's actions and feelings while in the forest?

2.  What changes took place in the character's feelings? Personality?

3.  How were these changes related to or reflected in the description of the forest?

4.  What does Hawthorne wish you to know about your character by his presentation in the forest scenes? How do you know this?

5. How has Hawthorne linked the forest scenes with his characters?

6. How has Hawthorne "manipulated" your reactions to his characters by placing them in the forest?

7. What are some associations you have with the forest?

8. Of what might Hawthorne's forest be symbolic?

9. In one sentence, describe a possible theme of the novel that was generated from your study of the forest.

# Lesson 7
## The End of the Labyrinth: Chapters 20–22

## Objectives

- To analyze the character of Dimmesdale in preparation for his confession
- To analyze how Hawthorne describes the four major characters in order to understand changes of attitude that have taken place
- To understand how the forest functions as both a physical setting and a spiritual power in the contrasting market place scenes

## Notes to the Teacher

This lesson brings the minister and the reader out of the labyrinth that Hawthorne has constructed. In fact, all the characters have descended into their own labyrinth, each emerging with varying results. You may want to recount the mythological legend of the Labyrinth of the Isle of Crete as a prelude to the handouts. These handouts "set the stage" for the final act and curtain of the drama through which Hawthorne has moved his characters in his "morality play."

## Procedure

1. Distribute **Handout 21.** Use as homework in the reading of Chapter 20 or as an in-class group assignment. Brainstorming after completion of Part I is useful for giving students a broad range of information.

   **Suggested Responses** Part II
   1. *Answers will vary depending on the work done on the chart.*
   2. *Answers will vary depending on work done on chart.*
   3. *Answers may vary, but students should see that Dimmesdale is vacillating between his obligations to himself, to Hester, and to the community.*

4. *Students should see how he has changed spiritually, prodded by his sojourn in the forest with Hester and Pearl and his encounters with various townspeople on his way home.*
5. *The fact that he is able to write his Election Day sermon is one indication.*

2. Distribute **Handout 22.** This handout asks the students to look at the changes in characters and setting, again as a prelude to the finale. It lends itself to either homework or small group work.

**Suggested Responses** Part II
1. *Answers will vary depending on the chart work.*
2. *Hester and Pearl are sympathetically presented. Dimmesdale is not. Reactions to the townspeople will vary, but the townspeople are not as harshly presented as in earlier chapters.*
3. *The contrasts in clothing add to the "festive" quality of the scene.*
4. *There is an air of the holiday, which is different from the "holiday" atmosphere in the earlier chapters.*
5. *The festive mood seems to be underscored.*
6. *By now students should see that the expectations and the moods are different. There is more of an acceptance of Hester's being in their midst.*
7. *They seem to accept each other more.*
8. *The characters have undergone their own "forest experience," confronting the "sin" that walks among them and responding or not responding to it in their own ways.*

9. *This is a speculative question, but students should guess that the final confession will take place.*

3. Distribute **Handout 23.** Its purpose is for students to see the major differences between the two uses of the market place and to realize its use as a symbol. They are also to comprehend how the forest becomes both a physical presence and a spiritual metaphor or symbol.

**Suggested Responses**

1. *Based on their work with **Handout 22** as well as this one, students will see the attitudinal changes reflected in the characters and their reasons for being in the market place. Thus, the description of a place is colored and shaped by the characters.*

2. *The characters have all confronted certain issues in their lives and are now coming together for different reasons.*

3. *They have lived with Hester among them and have responded to her many "works of mercy" and seem to have forgotten her "scarlet letter."*

4. *a. Hester—seems to be more at ease with herself, stronger as a person*

*b. Pearl—little, if any change*

*c. Dimmesdale—more open with himself about his role in Hester's sin*

*d. Chillingworth—hardened even more*

5. *Mistress Hibbins. To confront Hester with the darkness of sin. To remind the reader of the evil that is associated with the forest.*

6. *A place of evil and possibly a form of redemption.*

7. *By having the characters journey through the forest, Hawthorne may be showing that the market place no longer suggests the dread and animosity it once did since the major characters have suffered more than they did earlier in the market place.*

## Optional Activities

The handouts in this lesson are designed as groundwork for compositions. They can be used as pre-drafting exercises for either a comparison/contrast or an analysis paper.

Name _____

Date _____

# Un-Mazing Grace

Part I

**Directions:**

Re-read Chapter 20 carefully in order to fill in the following chart. Find specific words or phrases that fit the categories listed. After completing the chart, respond to the questions that follow it.

| Category | Peace | Terror/Dismay |
|---|---|---|
| **Natural Setting** | | |
| **Other Settings Details** | | |
| **Sense Imagery** | | |
| **Feelings** | | |
| **Social Setting** | | |

Part II

1.  What are the strongest image words used to create a sense of peace?
    (Select from each of the categories.)

2.  What are the strongest image words used to create a sense of dismay or terror? (Select
    from each of the categories.)

3.  What conclusions can you draw from these contrasting images?

4. What insight into Arthur Dimmesdale do you have at this point?

5. In what ways do the contrasting images seem to indicate that Dimmesdale has had a great burden lifted from his soul?

Name _____

Date _____

# Setting the Stage

Part I

**Directions:**
Re-read Chapters 21 and 22 carefully. Imagine that these chapters are two scenes from a movie. Try to visualize what is going on and what the settings and characters look like. Find words or phrases in these chapters to use in filling in the chart.

| | Physical Descriptions | Clothing Descriptions | Sense Imagery | Feelings |
|---|---|---|---|---|
| **Hester** | | | | |
| **Pearl** | | | | |
| **Dimmesdale** | | | | |

|  | Physical Descriptions | Clothing Descriptions | Sense Imagery | Feelings |
|---|---|---|---|---|
| **Chillingworth** | | | | |
| **Other Characters** | | | | |

Part II

1. Based on the physical descriptions of the characters, what does Hawthorne want you to think about them?

2. Which are more sympathetically presented? Which are not? Why is this so?

3. How do the clothing descriptions add to an understanding of the characters and their role?

4. How does the sense imagery set a tone?

5. What role do the feelings of the characters play in setting a tone?

6. In the opening chapters of the novel, there was a gathering of people as there is in these two chapters. What is different about the two gatherings?

7. What is different about the characters now as compared with the opening chapters?

8. Why is there this difference?

9. For what do you think Hawthorne is setting the stage? How do you know?

# The Forest and the Market Place

## Directions

Re-read the first three chapters and Chapters 21 and 22. You will notice that the market place is the central setting in these chapters. However, the forest now plays an important role in Chapters 21 and 22, so the two settings are merged. After you complete the following chart, please answer the questions that follow it.

|  | The Market Place Chapters 1–3 | The Market Place Chapters 21–22 |
|---|---|---|
| People Present In Market Place |  |  |
| Reasons for Being There |  |  |
| Attitudes Of Those Present |  |  |
| Major Sense Imagery Used in Description of Market Place |  |  |

1. What major differences do you see in the two descriptions of the market place?

2. Why have these changes taken place?

3. How are the characters, other than the four major characters, different?

4. While the forest is not physically present in the second presentation of the market place, it is spiritually present. The four major characters—Hester, Pearl, Dimmesdale, and Chillingworth—have all been in the forest at one time or another and for different reasons. How has this changed them?

   a. Hester

   b. Pearl

   c. Dimmesdale

   d. Chillingworth

5. What other character present in the market place is associated with the forest? Why is the character in the market place?

6. Recalling the work you did in Lesson 6 with **Handouts 19 and 20,** what is the spiritual power of the forest?

7. How has the forest affected the second presentation of the market place in Chapters 21 and 22 and thus affected all those present now?

# Lesson 8

## The Finale: Chapters 23–24

## Objective

- To critique the final chapters
- To demonstrate a division of the novel with the scaffold as the dividing symbol
- To establish the theme of isolation

## Notes to the Teacher

The handouts in this lesson ask students to look at the final chapters as though they were critics, evaluating certain things that Hawthorne did. They are asked to evaluate the purpose of Chapter 24 in light of the entire novel.

## Procedure

1. Distribute **Handout 24.** Allow some time for small group discussion so that students can respond to the questions. Follow with a class discussion, challenging defense of answers with proof from the novel.

   **Suggested Responses**
   1. *The scaffold acts as a physical division of the novel and as a symbol. It raises the characters to public view and shame.*
   2. *Answers will vary but challenge students to support their contentions with proof from the novel.*
   3. *Students should use the physical and affective descriptions Hawthorne provides in these chapters.*
   4. *The differences occur in the range of physical deterioration of the scaffold from the first three chapters to the last chapter. There is also the difference detailed in Dimmesdale's night-time visit to the scaffold.*
   5. *Students should comment on the public shame experienced by those who ascend the scaffold. (Note: Some students can research the history*

and use of the scaffold in Puritan towns and explain why it is located in the market place.)

2. Distribute **Handout 25.**

   **Suggested Responses**
   1. *She is despairing.*
   2. *This action tends to isolate her even more.*
   3. *(a) Hester: The townspeople move away from her and she is no closer to Pearl.*
      *(b) Pearl: Hester shuts her off from asking about Dimmesdale.*
      *(c) Dimmesdale: He has effectively withdrawn from his parishioners and, in a sense, is isolated from God.*
      *(d) Chillingworth: He no longer has a hold over Dimmesdale and, therefore, has no justification for his efforts.*
   4. *Answers will vary, but students should extract specific comments from the novel to support their contentions.*
   5. *Students should come to see how the characters have been isolated throughout the novel. This is an opportunity to present one of the traditional themes of Hawthorne—that of isolation's being the more serious "sin."*

3. Distribute **Handout 26.**

   **Suggested Responses**
   1. *Responses might indicate the tying up of loose ends.*
   2. *Details will come from the text.*
   3. *Indications of consistency should arise from understanding how the characters acted previously. This is a means of evaluating character actions and development.*
   4. *Answers will vary.*

# Climb Every Scaffold

**Directions**

Read the following commentary carefully and answer the questions that follow.

> [The separation of the novel] is built around the scaffold. At the beginning, in the middle, and at the end of the story the scaffold is the dominating point. Just as it literally rises above the market place, so does it structurally rise out of the novel's plan and attribute pattern to it. In Chapter 2, after the very short first chapter, Hester is taken up on the scaffold. In Chapter 12, the middle chapter (when we omit the concluding chapter), Dimmesdale mounts the scaffold. In Chapter 23, the last (which precedes the conclusion), Dimmesdale takes Hester and Pearl up there with him. These three incidents are, in every sense, the high points of the novel. Chapter 12 tends to divide the story into two parts (or three parts, counting this middle chapter). This division is logical when we realize that prior to Chapter 12, neither the reader nor Chillingworth is certain that Dimmesdale is the father of little Pearl; after Chapter 12, there can be no doubt.[1]

1. Based on the commentary, what is the importance of the scaffold in the novel?




2. Is the writer's contention that the scaffold divides the novel into two or three parts a valid one? Why or why not?










[1] Leland Schubert, *Hawthorne the Artist*, (Chapel Hill: University of North Carolina Press, 1944).

3. How is the scaffold described in the following chapters?

   (a) Chapters 1—3

   (b) Chapter 12

   (c) Chapter 23

4. What are the differences in these descriptions?

5. What is the symbolic use of the scaffold?

Name _____

Date _____

# In Full View

## Directions
Answer the following questions about Chapter 23.

1. How does Hester respond to Dimmesdale's asking her and Pearl to come up onto the scaffold with him?

2. Why do you think she feels this way?

3. Each of the following characters, rather than being united, is more isolated. Explain this isolation.

   (a) Hester

   (b) Pearl

   (c) Dimmesdale

   (d) Chillingworth

4. What specific evidence in the novel supports this sense of isolation for the characters?

   (a) Hester

   (b) Pearl

   (c) Dimmesdale

   (d) Chillingworth

5. Show how this sense of isolation is a possible theme for the novel.

Name _____

Date _____

# Conclusion

**Directions**
After reading Chapter 24 carefully, answer the following questions.

1. Some critics say that Chapter 23 is the actual end of the novel. If this is so, why do you think Hawthorne wrote Chapter 24?

2. How are the following characters described in Chapter 24?
   (a) Hester

   (b) Pearl

   (c) Dimmesdale

   (d) Chillingworth

3. How are these descriptions consistent with what has happened to the characters?

4. If you were writing this novel, how would you end it? Why?

# Lesson 9
## Symposium: The Novel As A Whole

## Objectives

- To present the results of the study of symbolism
- To present the results of the study of character development
- To view these elements in the context of the complete novel

## Notes to the Teacher

This lesson brings together elements of study done while students were reading the novel. Create a "community of scholars" who share their findings and insights. As indicated in the directions on **Handouts 1** and **2**, students are asked to present their findings in a variety of ways. By encouraging these approaches, a symposium atmosphere in the classroom can be created. **Handout 29** may be used to create a group paper (see Lesson 1 for suggestions), an individual paper, or some type of oral presentation. The important point is that all students are exposed to the full range of possibilities. If students do a paper, consider having a copy of each photo-copied as a collection of critical essays.

## Procedure

1. Distribute **Handout 27.** Ask students to convene in the groups first assigned.

**Suggested Responses**
1. *Answers will vary.*
2. *Answers will vary, but students should see how the symbol grows out of the context of the story and the actions of the characters.*
3. *Answers will vary.*
4. *Answers will vary.*
5. *Answers will vary.*
6. *Answers will vary.*
7. *Answers will vary.*

2. Distribute **Handout 28.** Ask students to convene in the groups first assigned.

**Suggested Responses**
*Answers will vary.*

3. Distribute **Handout 29.** This handout lends itself to small group work. There are six possible themes, but other themes of your choice may be added or substituted. There are options for acquainting the entire class with all the possible themes. Help students to understand that theme is an organic outgrowth of the novel, not an artificial imposition. They should also become aware that theme is not necessarily a story's moral as in an Aesop fable.

**Suggested Responses**
*Answers will vary.*

Name _____

Date _____

# The Symbol: A Means of Understanding

**Directions**

Refer to your work on **Handouts 5, 6, and 7.** Review the work and develop an accurate and concrete summary of your findings to present creatively to the class.

Assigned Symbol: _____

1. What stands out in your mind about the assigned symbol as you followed it throughout the novel? What is the significance of that symbol in relation to the novel?

2. How did this symbol weave itself into the texture of the novel?

3. How did the symbol help you to understand the story?

4.  Was your symbol in any way connected with any of the characters in the novel? Who? What was the connection? How did this connection help you to understand the character?

5.  What other conclusions and observations can you make about the symbol?

6.  What information and understanding of the novel can you share with the class based on your work with a symbol?

7.  What is the best method for presenting this information? Why is this the best way?

Name _____

Date _____

# Character Analysis

**Directions**

In **Handout 8,** you were assigned a character to follow throughout your reading of the novel. Review the charts you kept. Prepare a presentation of your study of this character.
Character Studied: _____

1. What were some of the character's significant actions as you followed him or her throughout the novel?

2. What insight did these actions provide into the personality of the character?

3. What were some of the most significant statements made by the character?

4. How did these statements provide you with insight into your character?

5. How did your character interact with other characters?

6. In the final analysis, how do you feel about your character? About your character's role in the story?

7. What information do you need to present to the rest of the class so that they will understand what you learned about this character?

8. What is the best way for you to present this information? Why?

Name _____

Date _____

# Theme: A Thread That Binds

## Directions

A theme of any story is a thread that runs throughout the story. In the case of a novel there may be several themes. Listed below are some of the themes that are commonly discussed in relation to *The Scarlet Letter.* Based on the knowledge you have acquired, work with the theme assigned to your group.

Possible Themes

1. The effects of guilt

2. The effects of sin

3. Isolation and alienation from self and society

4. Intolerance and non-forgiveness

5. Obsession for revenge

6. Suffering, punishment, and redemption

Assigned Theme _____

1. How is this theme demonstrated by the action of the characters? What character best demonstrates this theme? Why?

2. How do the symbols, both the conventional and non-clichéd, serve to underscore the theme? What symbol best demonstrates this theme? Why?

Name _____

Date _____

3. What aspect of setting best demonstrates the theme? How? Why?

4. How does the point of view allow you to see this as a theme for the novel?

5. How does the structure of the novel as presented in **Handout 24** help to understand this theme?

# Lesson 10
## The Novel as a Whole

## Objectives

- To use and evaluate schema for character analysis
- To challenge "critical" analyses
- To develop writing skills
- To test learning achievement

## Notes to the Teacher

This lesson is a potpourri of items. **Handout 30** presents a schema for analyzing the main characters. Since it is based on the four classical humors, supplement this work either with an explanation or assign research on the humors. **Handout 31** presents two bogus interpretations of the forest scenes. This lesson allows the students to challenge "authority" and to sharpen their critical and evaluative techniques. Do not inform them of the spurious aspect of the "criticisms" until the proper time. (See Procedure below.) There are also several topics which may be used as either individual or group compositions. Some of the topics may lend themselves to a short research paper. Several handouts may be used as either reading checks or as a unit test after completing the lessons.

## Procedure

1. Distribute **Handout 30.** Students may work in groups on this assignment.

   **Suggested Responses**
   1. *(a) Hester: blood; hot and moist; air (b) Pearl: phelgm; cold and moist; water (c) Dimmesdale: black bile; cold and dry; earth; (d) Chillingworth; yellow bile; hot and dry; fire,*
   2. *Answers will vary, but students should see the actions of Dimmesdale as being aligned closely with the Black Man and that there is a certain quality of melancholia in him. Chillingworth is closely aligned with fire as shown in the scene in* **Handout 11.**
   3. *Students should see that this may be a valid, although artificial, device. Guide them through the use of this device without going to extremes.*

2. Distribute **Handout 31.** Allow students full responsibility for this assignment. Use the inclination to believe anything in print as gospel, to have fun with this handout. After the first three questions are answered, then answer question 4 in writing before holding a class discussion. This will provide an opportunity to distinguish between a legitimate interpretation that is supported by the text and one that is merely suggested by text. This is a good time to make a point about scholarship and basing opinion on fact and knowledge.

   **Suggested Responses**
   *Answers will vary.*

3. Distribute **Handout 32.** Students may choose their own topics for this assignment. If it is to be a group paper, refer to instructions in Lesson 1.

4. Distribute **Handout 33.** This handout may be used as reading check on assigned chapters or as part of a final test.

## Suggested Responses

1. This chapter is mainly a mood-setter. There are aspects of ugliness, the setting of the prison and cemetery, and the rose bush.
2. The Puritan society condemns Hester without admitting its own sinfulness.
3. Hester is filled with dread, horror, and steadfastness.
4. Chillingworth: lonely, gentle, determined
   Hester: uncaring toward Chillingworth, loving toward Dimmesdale
5. It gives her some contact with the community. She does nothing for weddings since the Puritans would see this as hypocritical in view of her sin.
6. She is uncontrollable, intelligent, emotional, impish. By her actions with other children, her imagination, and descriptions the narrator provides.

5. Distribute **Handout 34.** This handout may be used as a reading check or as part of a final test.

## Suggested Responses

1. The breastplate reflects the scarlet "A" and magnifies it. Pearl is also reflected in the breastplate.
2. He establishes the relationships among the four characters.
3. Chillingworth becomes more evil, which was hinted at by his relationship with Dimmesdale.
4. Chillingworth is vicious and merciless. Dimmesdale is passive, especially as he sleeps under the doctor's scrutiny.
5. The more he tries to admit his sinfulness, the more the townsfolk admire his holiness. He does not strongly try to dispel this attitude.
6. Dimmesdale stands alone on the scaffold, agonizing over his part in the sin that has condemned Hester to wear the scarlet letter. The reader is shown the depth of Dimmesdale's grief.

6. Distribute **Handout 35.** This handout may be used as reading check or as part of a final test.

## Suggested Responses

1. To relieve the tension of Chapter 12 and to further the development of the characters.
2. Chillingworth's discussion with Hester brings out both feelings.
3. He shows her playing along the seashore and we see by her games the depth of both her intellect and her imagination. We see her through Hester's eyes in order to understand Hester's concern for her.
4. Answers will vary.
5. This is the first time they have been alone together and we see them as lovers.
6. Nature is in control.
7. She rejects his attempts at closeness.

7. Distribute **Handout 36.** This handout may be used as reading check or as part of a final test.

## Suggested Responses

1. He becomes openly scornful of the Puritan ways and seems to submit to sin.
2. Their suppression of joy, even on a joyous occasion; somber dress contrasted with the bright clothing of the Indians and sailors.
3. He must reveal himself to the townspeople; we see his struggle in deciding to do so.
4. Dimmesdale asks Hester and Pearl to join him on the scaffold. He then admits his role in Hester's sin.
5. To update the reader with the outcome of the characters after the plot ends.

# Character Analysis

**Directions**
Read the following about the humors, first discussed by Hippocrates. Answer the questions that follow.

Hippocrates, a fourth century Greek, explained human disease on the basis of four humors. These were *Blood* which originated in the heart; *phlegm,* which originated in the brain; *black bile,* or melancholia, which originated in the spleen; and *yellow bile,* or cholera, which originated in the liver. These humors were associated with other elements as follows:

Blood . . . . . . . . . . . . . . . . air . . . . . . . . . . . . . . . . . . hot and moist

Yellow bile . . . . . . . . . . . . fire . . . . . . . . . . . . . . . . . . hot and dry

Phlegm . . . . . . . . . . . . . . water . . . . . . . . . . . . . . . cold and moist

Black bile . . . . . . . . . . . . earth . . . . . . . . . . . . . . . . cold and dry

This concept of using humors as a basis for understanding disease also became the basis for understanding human personality. This theory continued well into the nineteenth century, so it is likely that Hawthorne was aware of the humors and their relevance to medicine and psychology of his time.

1. Based on this brief description of the four humors, which seem to dominate the following characters?

    a. Hester:

    b. Pearl:

    c. Dimmesdale:

    d. Chillingworth:

2. What actions of the main characters seem to be consistent with their associated humors?

   a. Hester:

   b. Pearl:

   c. Dimmesdale:

   d. Chillingworth:

3. Is this a valid device for understanding and describing these characters? Why or why not?

Name _____

Date _____

# Interpreting the Novel

## Directions

Many critics have analyzed this novel, its characters, its symbols, and its themes. Now, you are to assume a critic's role to evaluate critical analyses of others. Re-read Chapters 16 to 19 carefully. Read the comments by critics (below) and respond to the questions that follow.

## Selection 1

. . . [A]s we have seen, the forest is an archetypal symbol of both the fall and the redemption. The Edenic Tree endowed both Adam and Eve with knowledge, albeit knowledge that led to their expulsion from Paradise. In *The Scarlet Letter* we are again confronted with Hawthorne's obsession with the use of forests and trees as a central motif. This time, however, the forest takes on the symbolic significance of redemption and freedom. Both Hester and Dimmesdale are shown sitting on a fallen tree, a tree of antiquity, a tree covered with moss. Might Hawthorne be directing us to consider this tree the Tree of Eden, fallen and waiting for a new Adam and Eve? This is not without merit since we see them both joyous later as the sunlight streams in on them.

The Eden story places it near water, at the joining of three rivers. Hawthorne has his new Adam and Eve sitting near a stream with which Pearl is fascinated. Again, as I mentioned before, the Jungian concept of the search for the father leading to water is repeated. In this case, the "father" concept is severalfold. It is the "father" for whom Pearl is searching—the man sitting with Hester. It is the "father" for whom Dimmesdale is searching—the authority to free himself. And finally, it is the "father" for whom Hester is searching. She, however, is looking for the "father" or Jungian "Animus" within herself.[1]

## Selection 2

. . . Cordell's contention of the New Eden is not without merit, but the central symbol of the forest must be seen within the context of the Hawthorne canon. While Hawthorne freely uses Biblical allusions and imagery, we cannot allow the forest to be so narrowly interpreted. Schematic study of his short story, "My Kinsman, Major Molineaux," shows the preoccupation Hawthorne has with the founding of a new country, separating itself from the "Mother Country," replete with growing pains and separation anxieties. In *The Scarlet Letter*, we see the forest as the wilderness, not the Eden Cordell found. Hester may be the new Eve, but she is the new Eve of the new country. Chillingworth represents the deterioration of the values of the Old World in the midst of the new. Dimmesdale is analogous to the new Adam who is not completed until he encounters his new Eve. She leads to his redemption, his growth, instead of to his downfall.

So the forest is not Edenic, not the blissful place of redemption as Cordell contends. It is the birthing place of a new spirit, found in both Hester and Pearl. And, therefore, it is the new country coming to fruition.[2]

[1]Vance Cordell, *Man in Retrograde Motion* (Parson College Press, 1967), 31–34

[2]Sharon Gowanda, *The American Myths of Hawthorne* (University of Wallensburg Press, 1968), 14–17.

1.  Based on your reading and working with *The Scarlet Letter,* do you agree with the interpretation that Cordell makes in passage 1? Why or why not?

2.  Do you agree with Gowanda's interpretation? Why or why not?

3. Write your own interpretation of the same chapters. Support with specific references.

4. At this point, you will learn something about this handout. Write your response to this information.

# Topics for Composition

**Directions**

You are to write a well-reasoned, well-organized composition based on one of the topics below.

Topic 1

Select one of the major characters from *The Scarlet Letter*. Write an article for the school newspaper showing how that character's inner state of being or state of mind is reflected in a specific setting of the novel.

Topic 2

Select a symbol that proved to be especially significant to understanding the novel. In a paper written for someone who has not yet read the novel, explain how your understanding of the action of the novel or of a particular character was aided by this symbol.

Topic 3

Select one of the novel's major characters and explain how the narrator felt about the person. You are to write this paper for a classmate who has read the novel but does not fully understand the importance of point of view. Cite specific examples from the novel to support your position.

Topic 4

Critics debate who committed the greater sin, Hester, Chillingworth, or Dimmesdale. Based on your understanding of the novel, explain your choice of the person who committed the greater sin to a classmate who disagrees. Support your position with specific proof.

Topic 5

You have been asked to write an article for a literary magazine in which you demonstrate the relevance of a work written in the 1800s in today's society. Using *The Scarlet Letter* as a basis for this article, show how it is meaningful to the modern world.

Topic 6

Minor characters in a novel are just as important as the major characters. They may not be as fully drawn, but they contribute to the overall purpose of the story. Assume that your teacher does not agree with this. Select any three minor characters from *The Scarlet Letter* and present an argument in which you demonstrate their importance for a fuller understanding of the novel.

Topic 7

You are a contemporary of Hawthorne and have just finished reading his new novel, *The Scarlet Letter*. You are also a writer, have had several stories published, and are writing a novel. You do, however, have a problem with the point of view that Hawthorne has chosen for the novel. You also dislike the editorial intrusion of the narrator. Write a letter to Hawthorne explaining how a different point of view could improve the story.

Topic 8

One critic has said that Hawthorne seems to write a story as if it were a dream. A classmate disagrees with this. Write a rebuttal to this classmate's position in which you demonstrate that *The Scarlet Letter* has a dream-like quality. Support your position with proof.

Topic 9

In working with *The Scarlet Letter* you have learned that literary criticism is a special talent. You have also learned that you must be able to support your criticism with references to the text and be able to view matters like symbols within the context of the story. A classmate does not agree. This person believes that whatever one says about a story is true because "it's my opinion." In your paper, show that this approach is invalid. Explain the value of intelligent literary criticism and demonstrate by selecting a passage from the novel and interpreting it.

Name _____

Date _____

# Reading Check: Chapters 1–6

**Directions**
Answer the following questions.

1. What is the purpose of Chapter 1? Explain.

2. In Chapter 2, Hawthorne presents a sampling of the Puritan society. Describe the attitudes of this society toward Hester and Pearl.

3. In Chapter 3, Hester and Pearl stand on the scaffold in the market place. How would you best describe Hester's attitude as she stands there?

4. In Chapter 4, Chillingworth and Hester talk in her prison cell. How would you describe each of them?

    Chillingworth:

    Hester:

5. In Chapter 5, explain the importance of Hester's needlework. Why do you think she is not asked to sew for weddings?

6. In Chapter 6, what is the reader's impression of Pearl? How do you know this?

# Reading Check: Chapters 7–12

**Directions**
Answer the following questions.

1. Explain how the breastplate of the suit of armor and Pearl help to define the symbol of the scarlet "A" in Chapter 7.

2. What is the importance of Chapter 8 as Hawthorne brings together his four major characters?

3. What changes do you notice in Chillingworth in Chapter 9? How have these changes been foreshadowed in previous chapters?

4. How is Chillingworth described in Chapter 10? How does Hawthorne create a contrast to describe him?

5. What is the irony of Reverend Dimmesdale's public confession of sinfulness in Chapter 11? How does he take advantage of this?

6. How does the second scaffold scene in Chapter 12 help the reader to focus on Dimmesdale? What is the psychological impact of this scene?

Name _____

Date _____

# Reading Check: Chapters 13–19

**Directions**
Answer the following questions.

1. What are two possible reasons for Chapter 13?

2. How does Hawthorne present Chillingworth as a character worthy of sympathy as well as condemnation in Chapter 14?

3. How does Hawthorne develop Pearl in Chapter 15? Why does he have the reader view Pearl through Hester's eyes?

4. Select two symbols from Chapter 16, and explain their significance to the chapter and to the novel.

5. What makes Chapter 17 unique regarding the characters of Hester and Dimmesdale?

6. What use does Hawthorne make of nature in Chapter 18?

7. What is the symbolic significance in Chapter 19, of Pearl's washing away Dimmesdale's kiss?

Name _____

Date _____

# Reading Check: Chapters 20–24

**Directions**

Answer the following questions.

1. In Chapter 20, how has Dimmesdale changed?

2. In Chapter 21, what do you learn about Puritan society? What contrasts does Hawthorne use to portray that society?

3. In Chapter 22, what is the importance of focusing on Dimmesdale?

4. In Chapter 23, how does the third scaffold scene bring Dimmesdale's struggle to a conclusion?

5. What is the main purpose of Chapter 24?

# Acknowledgments

For permission to reprint all works in this volume by each of the following authors, grateful acknowledgment is made to the holders of copyright, publishers, or representatives named below.

Lesson 2, Handout 4
"What Started Walking Home From School" from *The Man Who Kept Cigars In His Cap.* (c) 1979 by Jim Heynen. Reprinted by permission of Graywolf Press, St. Paul, Minnesota.

Lesson 2, 4, 5, Handout 3, 10, 11, 16
Excerpts from *The Scarlet Letter* by Nathaniel Hawthorne, 1979. Published by The Perfection Form Co., Logan, Iowa.

Lesson 3, Handout 6
Adaptation from *Dynamics Of Faith* by Paul Tillich, 1957. Published by Harper & Row Publishers, Inc., New York, New York.

Lesson 5, 6, Handout 14, 17
Excerpts from *The Process of Fiction*, edited by Barbara McKenzie, copyright (c) 1969 by Harcourt Brace Jovanovich, Inc. Reprinted by permission of the publisher.

Lesson 8, Handout 24
Excerpt from *Hawthorne, The Artist: Fine-Art Devices in Fiction*, by Leland Schubert. (c) 1944 The University of North Carolina Press, Reprinted by permission.

**NOVEL/DRAMA**

**CURRICULUM UNITS**

# Novel/Drama Series

## Novel

*Absolutely Normal Chaos/*
*Chasing Redbird,* Creech

*Across Five Aprils,* Hunt

*Adam of the Road,* Gray/*Catherine,*
*Called Birdy,* Cushman

*The Adventures of Huckleberry*
*Finn,* Twain

*The Adventures of Tom Sawyer,*
Twain

*Alice's Adventures in Wonderland/*
*Through the Looking-Glass,*
Carroll

*All Creatures Great and Small,*
Herriot

*All Quiet on the Western Front,*
Remarque

*All the King's Men,* Warren

*Animal Farm,* Orwell/
*The Book of the Dun Cow,*
Wangerin, Jr.

*Anna Karenina,* Tolstoy

*Anne Frank: The Diary of a Young*
*Girl,* Frank

*Anne of Green Gables,* Montgomery

*April Morning,* Fast

*The Assistant/The Fixer,* Malamud

*The Autobiography of Miss Jane*
*Pittman,* Gaines

*The Awakening,* Chopin/
*Madame Bovary,* Flaubert

*Babbitt,* Lewis

*The Bean Trees/Pigs in Heaven,*
Kingsolver

*Beowulf/Grendel,* Gardner

*Billy Budd/Moby Dick,* Melville

*Black Boy,* Wright

*Bless Me, Ultima,* Anaya

*Brave New World,* Huxley

*The Bridge of San Luis Rey,* Wilder

*The Brothers Karamazov,*
Dostoevsky

*The Call of the Wild/White Fang,*
London

*The Canterbury Tales,* Chaucer

*The Catcher in the Rye,* Salinger

*The Cay/Timothy of the Cay,* Taylor

*Charlotte's Web,* White/
*The Secret Garden,* Burnett

*The Chosen,* Potok

*The Christmas Box,* Evans/
*A Christmas Carol,* Dickens

*Chronicles of Narnia,* Lewis

*Cold Sassy Tree,* Burns

*The Color of Water: A Black Man's*
*Tribute to His White Mother,*
McBride

*The Count of Monte Cristo,* Dumas

*Crime and Punishment,* Dostoevsky

*Cry, the Beloved Country,* Paton

*Dandelion Wine,* Bradbury

*Darkness at Noon,* Koestler

*David Copperfield,* Dickens

*Davita's Harp,* Potok

*A Day No Pigs Would Die,* Peck

*Death Comes for the Archbishop,*
Cather

*December Stillness,* Hahn/
*Izzy, Willy-Nilly,* Voigt

*The Divine Comedy,* Dante

*The Dollmaker,* Arnow

*Don Quixote,* Cervantes

*Dr. Zhivago,* Pasternak

*Dubliners,* Joyce

*East of Eden,* Steinbeck

*The Egypt Game,* Snyder/
*The Bronze Bow,* Speare

*Ellen Foster/A Virtuous Woman,*
Gibbons

*Emma,* Austen

*Fahrenheit 451,* Bradbury

*A Farewell to Arms,* Hemingway

*Farewell to Manzanar,* Houston &
Houston/*Black Like Me,* Griffin

*Frankenstein,* Shelley

*From the Mixed-up Files of Mrs.*
*Basil E. Frankweiler,*
Konigsburg/*The Westing Game,*
Raskin

*A Gathering of Flowers,* Thomas, ed.

*The Giver,* Lowry

*The Good Earth,* Buck

*The Grapes of Wrath,* Steinbeck

*Great Expectations,* Dickens

*The Great Gatsby,* Fitzgerald

*Gulliver's Travels,* Swift

*Hard Times,* Dickens

*Hatchet,* Paulsen/*Robinson Crusoe,*
Defoe

*Having Our Say,* Delany, Delany,
and Hearth/
*A Gathering of Old Men,* Gaines

*The Heart Is a Lonely Hunter,*
McCullers

*Heart of Darkness,* Conrad

*Hiroshima,* Hersey/*On the Beach,*
Shute

*The Hobbit,* Tolkien

*Homecoming/Dicey's Song,* Voigt

*The Hound of the Baskervilles,*
Doyle

*The Human Comedy/*
*My Name Is Aram,* Saroyan

*Incident at Hawk's Hill,* Eckert/
*Where the Red Fern Grows,*
Rawls

*Invisible Man,* Ellison

*Jane Eyre,* Brontë

*Johnny Tremain,* Forbes

*Journey of the Sparrows,* Buss and
Cubias/*The Honorable Prison,* de
Jenkins

*The Joy Luck Club,* Tan

*Jubal Sackett/The Walking Drum,*
L'Amour

*Julie of the Wolves,* George/*Island*
*of the Blue Dolphins,* O'Dell

*The Jungle,* Sinclair

*The Killer Angels,* Shaara

*Le Morte D'Arthur,* Malory

*The Learning Tree,* Parks

*Les Miserables,* Hugo

*The Light in the Forest/*
*A Country of Strangers,* Richter

*Little House in the Big Woods/*
*Little House on the Prairie,*
Wilder

*Little Women,* Alcott

*Lord of the Flies,* Golding

*The Lord of the Rings,* Tolkien

*The Martian Chronicles,* Bradbury

*Missing May,* Rylant/*The Summer*
*of the Swans,* Byars

*Mrs. Mike,* Freedman/*I Heard the*
*Owl Call My Name,* Craven

*Murder on the Orient Express/*
*And Then There Were None,*
Christie

*My Antonia,* Cather

*The Natural,* Malamud/*Shoeless*
*Joe,* Kinsella

*Nectar in a Sieve,* Markandaya/
*The Woman Warrior,* Kingston

*Night,* Wiesel

*A Night to Remember,* Lord/
*Streams to the River, River to the*
*Sea,* O'Dell

*1984,* Orwell

*Number the Stars,* Lowry/*Friedrich,*
Richter

*Obasan,* Kogawa

*The Odyssey,* Homer

*The Old Man and the Sea,*
Hemingway/*Ethan Frome,*
Wharton

*The Once and Future King,* White

*O Pioneers!*, Cather/*The Country of the Pointed Firs*, Jewett

*Ordinary People*, Guest/*The Tin Can Tree*, Tyler

*The Outsiders*, Hinton/*Durango Street*, Bonham

*The Pearl/Of Mice and Men*, Steinbeck

*The Picture of Dorian Gray*, Wilde/*Dr. Jekyll and Mr. Hyde*, Stevenson

*The Pigman/The Pigman's Legacy*, Zindel

*A Portrait of the Artist as a Young Man*, Joyce

*The Power and the Glory*, Greene

*A Prayer for Owen Meany*, Irving

*Pride and Prejudice*, Austen

*The Prince*, Machiavelli/*Utopia*, More

*The Prince and the Pauper*, Twain

*Profiles in Courage*, Kennedy

*Rebecca*, du Maurier

*The Red Badge of Courage*, Crane

*Red Sky at Morning*, Bradford

*The Return of the Native*, Hardy

*A River Runs Through It*, Maclean

*Roll of Thunder, Hear My Cry/Let the Circle Be Unbroken*, Taylor

*Saint Maybe*, Tyler

*Sarum*, Rutherfurd

*The Scarlet Letter*, Hawthorne

*The Scarlet Pimpernel*, Orczy

*A Separate Peace*, Knowles

*Shabanu: Daughter of the Wind/Haveli*, Staples

*Shane*, Schaefer/*The Ox-Bow Incident*, Van Tilburg Clark

*Siddhartha*, Hesse

*The Sign of the Chrysanthemum/The Master Puppeteer*, Paterson

*The Signet Classic Book of Southern Short Stories*, Abbott and Koppelman, eds.

*Silas Marner*, Eliot/*The Elephant Man*, Sparks

*The Slave Dancer*, Fox/*I, Juan de Pareja*, De Treviño

*Snow Falling on Cedars*, Guterson

*Song of Solomon*, Morrison

*The Sound and the Fury*, Faulkner

*Spoon River Anthology*, Masters

*A Stranger Is Watching/I'll Be Seeing You*, Higgins Clark

*The Stranger/The Plague*, Camus

*Summer of My German Soldier*, Greene/*Waiting for the Rain*, Gordon

*A Tale of Two Cities*, Dickens

*Talking God/A Thief of Time*, Hillerman

*Tess of the D'Urbervilles*, Hardy

*Their Eyes Were Watching God*, Hurston

*Things Fall Apart/No Longer at Ease*, Achebe

*To Kill a Mockingbird*, Lee

*To the Lighthouse*, Woolf

*Travels with Charley*, Steinbeck

*Treasure Island*, Stevenson

*A Tree Grows in Brooklyn*, Smith

*Tuck Everlasting*, Babbitt/*Bridge to Terabithia*, Paterson

*The Turn of the Screw/Daisy Miller*, James

*Uncle Tom's Cabin*, Stowe

*Walden*, Thoreau/*A Different Drummer*, Kelley

*Walk Two Moons*, Creech

*Walkabout*, Marshall

*Watership Down*, Adams

*The Watsons Go to Birmingham—1963*, Curtis/*The View from Saturday*, Konigsburg

*When the Legends Die*, Borland

*Where the Lilies Bloom*, Cleaver/*No Promises in the Wind*, Hunt

*Winesburg, Ohio*, Anderson

*The Witch of Blackbird Pond*, Speare/*My Brother Sam Is Dead*, Collier and Collier

*A Wrinkle in Time*, L'Engle/*The Lion, the Witch and the Wardrobe*, Lewis

*Wuthering Heights*, Brontë

*The Yearling*, Rawlings/*The Red Pony*, Steinbeck

*Year of Impossible Goodbyes*, Choi/*So Far from the Bamboo Grove*, Watkins

*Zlata's Diary*, Filipović/*The Lottery Rose*, Hunt

**Drama**

*Antigone*, Sophocles

*Arms and the Man/Saint Joan*, Shaw

*The Crucible*, Miller

*Cyrano de Bergerac*, Rostand

*Death of a Salesman*, Miller

*A Doll's House/Hedda Gabler*, Ibsen

*The Glass Menagerie*, Williams

*The Importance of Being Earnest*, Wilde

*Inherit the Wind*, Lawrence and Lee

*Long Day's Journey into Night*, O'Neill

*A Man for All Seasons*, Bolt

*Medea*, Euripides/*The Lion in Winter*, Goldman

*The Miracle Worker*, Gibson

*Murder in the Cathedral*, Eliot/*Galileo*, Brecht

*The Night Thoreau Spent in Jail*, Lawrence and Lee

*Oedipus the King*, Sophocles

*Our Town*, Wilder

*The Playboy of the Western World/Riders to the Sea*, Synge

*Pygmalion*, Shaw

*A Raisin in the Sun*, Hansberry

*1776*, Stone and Edwards

*She Stoops to Conquer*, Goldsmith/*The Matchmaker*, Wilder

*A Streetcar Named Desire*, Williams

*Tartuffe*, Molière

*Three Comedies of American Family Life: I Remember Mama*, van Druten/*Life with Father*, Lindsay and Crouse/*You Can't Take It with You*, Hart and Kaufman

*Waiting for Godot*, Beckett/*Rosencrantz & Guildenstern Are Dead*, Stoppard

**Shakespeare**

*As You Like It*

*Hamlet*

*Henry IV, Part I*

*Henry V*

*Julius Caesar*

*King Lear*

*Macbeth*

*The Merchant of Venice*

*A Midsummer Night's Dream*

*Much Ado about Nothing*

*Othello*

*Richard III*

*Romeo and Juliet*

*The Taming of the Shrew*

*The Tempest*

*Twelfth Night*

**The Center for Learning**

To Order Contact: **The Center for Learning—Shipping/Business Office**
P.O. Box 910 • Villa Maria, PA 16155
800-767-9090 • 724-964-8083 • Fax 888-767-8080

# The Publisher

All instructional materials identified by the TAP® (Teachers/Authors/Publishers) trademark are developed by a national network of teachers whose collective educational experience distinguishes the publishing objective of The Center for Learning, a nonprofit educational corporation founded in 1970.

Concentrating on values-related disciplines, the Center publishes humanities and religion curriculum units for use in public and private schools and other educational settings. Approximately 500 language arts, social studies, novel/drama, life issues, and faith publications are available.

While acutely aware of the challenges and uncertain solutions to growing educational problems, the Center is committed to quality curriculum development and to the expansion of learning opportunities for all students. Publications are regularly evaluated and updated to meet the changing and diverse needs of teachers and students. Teachers may offer suggestions for development of new publications or revisions of existing titles by contacting

## The Center for Learning

Administrative/Editorial Office
21590 Center Ridge Road
Rocky River, OH 44116
(440) 331-1404 • FAX (440) 331-5414
**E-mail:** cfl@stratos.net
**Web:** www.centerforlearning.org

For a free catalog containing order and price information and a descriptive listing of titles, contact

## The Center for Learning

Shipping/Business Office
P.O. Box 910
Villa Maria, PA 16155
(724) 964-8083 • (800) 767-9090
FAX (888) 767-8080

# Educator's Evaluation

The Center for Learning concept calls for updates. Teachers writing for teachers will give us the best in instructional material.

**Curriculum Unit Title**

| Excellent | Good | Fair | Poor | Criteria |
|-----------|------|------|------|----------|
| | | | | Overall effectiveness of the unit |
| | | | | Usability of the unit |
| | | | | Pacing of the material |
| | | | | Quality of format and layout |
| | | | | Availability of the selected text materials |
| | | | | Student evaluation of the material |
| | | | | Student motivation and interest |
| | | | | Ability level of students |
| | | | | Student achievement in the unit |

What is the greatest strength of this unit?

Used in Grade(s) _____

Used for
❏ Basic/Core for instruction
❏ Selected use
❏ Supplemental use

What would you change in this unit?

Teacher's experience
❏ 0–5 years
❏ 6–10 years
❏ 11–15 years
❏ 16 or more years

Additional Comments:

School Location
❏ large city
❏ suburb
❏ small town
❏ country

Name _____

Position _____

School _____

Address _____

School Enrollment
❏ 1–499 students
❏ 500–999 students
❏ 1000 or more students

Please return to:

**CL** The Center for Learning
21590 Center Ridge Rd.
Rocky River, OH 44116